Presented to:

_____

From:

_____

Date:

_____

Jesus Calling®

FOR

Easter

Sarah Young

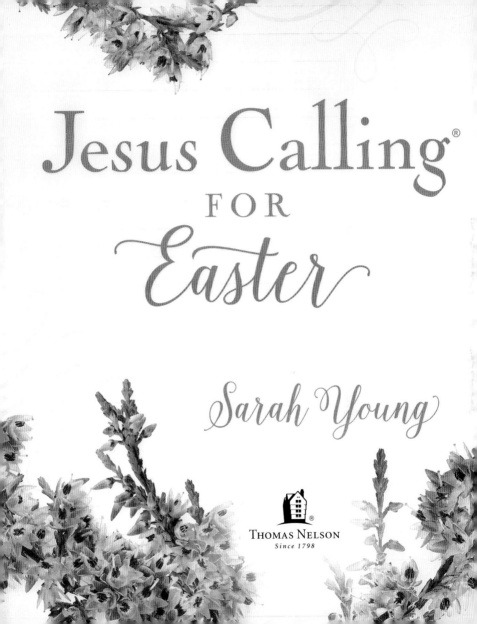

THOMAS NELSON
Since 1798

Jesus Calling for Easter

© 2020 Sarah Young

Published in Nashville, Tennessee, by Thomas Nelson. Thomas Nelson is a registered trademark of HarperCollins Christian Publishing, Inc.

Unless otherwise noted, Scripture quotations are taken from the Holy Bible, New International Version®, NIV®. Copyright © 1973, 1978, 1984 by Biblica, Inc.® Used by permission of Zondervan. All rights reserved worldwide. www.zondervan.com. The "NIV" and "New International Version" are trademarks registered in the United States Patent and Trademark Office by Biblica, Inc.®

Scripture quotations marked AMP are taken from the Amplified® Bible. Copyright © 1954, 1958, 1962, 1964, 1965, 1987 by The Lockman Foundation. Used by permission. www.Lockman.org

Scripture quotations marked ESV are taken from the ESV® Bible (The Holy Bible, English Standard Version®). Copyright © 2001 by Crossway, a publishing ministry of Good News Publishers. Used by permission. All rights reserved.

Scripture quotations marked KJV are taken from the King James Version. Public domain.

Scripture quotations marked NASB are taken from New American Standard Bible®. Copyright © 1960, 1962, 1963, 1968, 1971, 1972, 1973, 1975, 1977, 1995 by The Lockman Foundation. Used by permission. www.Lockman.org

Scripture quotations marked NKJV are taken from the New King James Version®. Copyright © 1982 by Thomas Nelson. Used by permission. All rights reserved.

Scripture quotations marked TLB are taken from The Living Bible. Copyright © 1971 by permission of Tyndale House Publishers, Inc., Carol Stream, Illinois 60188. All rights reserved.

Scripture quotations marked NLT are taken from the Holy Bible, New Living Translation. Copyright © 1996, 2004, 2015 by Tyndale House Foundation. Used by permission of Tyndale House Publishers, Inc., Carol Stream, Illinois 60188. All rights reserved.

Library of Congress Cataloging-in-Publication Data

ISBN 978-1-4002-1508-9 (audiobook)
ISBN 978-1-4002-1511-9 (eBook)
ISBN 978–1–4002–1510–2 (HC)

Printed in China

23 24 25 26 DSC 7 6 5 4

Dear Reader,

I believe the message of hope is extremely important at this time—for people throughout the US and around the world. May the pages of this book help you enjoy both the refreshing beauty of springtime and the wondrous glory of Jesus' supreme sacrifice on the cross. He paid the penalty for all the sins of everyone who trusts Him as Savior. So we can know that we are fully forgiven and that ultimately our story finishes well—at the portals of heaven! As we celebrate Christ's glorious resurrection, let us be assured that God is in control and He is good.

The devotions in this book are written from the perspective of Jesus speaking to you, the reader. I have included Scripture with each devotion, and I encourage you to read both—slowly and prayerfully.

I will be praying for readers of *Jesus Calling for Easter*. For any of you who do not yet know Jesus as Savior, I'll be asking God to bring you into His family of believers.

Remember that Jesus is with you at all times. May you enjoy His presence and His peace in ever-increasing measure.

Sarah Young

I am *overwhelmed* with joy in the LORD my God! For he has dressed me with the clothing of salvation and draped me in a robe of *righteousness*. I am like a bridegroom dressed for his wedding or a bride with her *jewels*.

—ISAIAH 61:10 NLT

I DELIGHT IN BRIGHTENING your perspective. That's why I ventured into your world, knowing full well the terrible price I would pay. I came *to open eyes that are blind, to free captives from prison, and to release from the dungeon those who sit in darkness.* When you find yourself imprisoned by ingratitude, ask Me to open your eyes and release you from that dark place.

You live in an age of entitlement, so you need to counteract the messages proclaiming that you deserve more. One way is to jot down some things you're thankful for each day. This changes your focus from things you wish you had to blessings you already have.

Saturating your mind with Scripture can help you see from My infinitely wise perspective. My Word is *sharper than any double-edged sword*; I use it to perform spiritual surgery on *the thoughts and attitudes of your heart.* As Scripture lights up your point of view, I set you free from the dungeon of ingratitude, releasing you to enjoy the pleasures of a thankful heart.

".. . to open eyes that are blind, to free
captives from prison and to release from
the dungeon those who sit in darkness."

ISAIAH 42:7

For the word of God is living and active. Sharper
than any double-edged sword, it penetrates even
to dividing soul and spirit, joints and marrow; it
judges the thoughts and attitudes of the heart.

HEBREWS 4:12

Your word is a lamp to my feet
and a light for my path.

PSALM 119:105

You have made *known* to me the path of life; you will *fill* me with *joy* in your presence, with eternal *pleasures* at your right hand.

PSALM 16:11

*T*HERE IS AN OPEN ROAD AHEAD OF YOU—all the way to heaven. I am your traveling Companion, and I know every twist and turn of your path. You see problems and limitations impeding your progress no matter which direction you look. But your vision is ever so limited. All I ask of you is to take the next small step—refusing to give up, refusing to stop trusting Me.

Your life is truly a faith-walk, and I am absolutely faithful! Though your understanding will fail you, I never will. The challenge before you is to stop focusing on your problems and limitations—and to believe that the way ahead really is an open road, in spite of how it looks.

I am the Way to the Father in heaven. Remember how much I had to suffer in order to open up *the path of Life* for you. No one else will ever have to endure what I went through. When you are struggling, simply take the next step and thank Me for clearing the way before you—all the way to heaven.

No temptation has seized you except what is common to man. And God is faithful; he will not let you be tempted beyond what you can bear. But when you are tempted, he will also provide a way out so that you can stand up under it.

1 CORINTHIANS 10:13

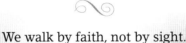

We walk by faith, not by sight.

2 CORINTHIANS 5:7 NKJV

Jesus said to [Thomas], "I am the way, the truth, and the life. No one comes to the Father except through Me."

JOHN 14:6 NKJV

Thanks be to *God* for His *indescribable* gift!

2 CORINTHIANS 9:15 NKJV

I WANT YOU TO EXPERIENCE the riches of your salvation: the Joy of being loved constantly and perfectly. You make a practice of judging yourself based on how you look or behave or feel. If you like what you see in the mirror, you feel a bit more worthy of My Love. When things are going smoothly and your performance seems adequate, you find it easier to believe you are My beloved child. When you feel discouraged, you tend to look inward so you can correct whatever is wrong.

Instead of trying to "fix" yourself, *fix your gaze on Me, the Lover of your soul*. Rather than using your energy to judge yourself, redirect it to praising Me. Remember that I see you clothed in My righteousness, radiant in My perfect Love.

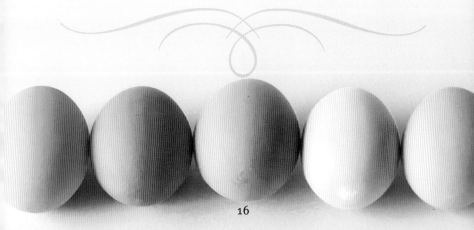

In order that in the coming ages he might show the incomparable riches of his grace, expressed in his kindness to us in Christ Jesus. For it is by grace you have been saved, through faith—and this not from yourselves, it is the gift of God.

EPHESIANS 2:7–8

Therefore, holy brothers, who share in the heavenly calling, fix your thoughts on Jesus, the apostle and high priest whom we confess.

HEBREWS 3:1

Those who look to him are radiant; their faces are never covered with shame.

PSALM 34:5

I AM THE ONE AND ONLY *who came from the Father, full of grace and truth.* I came from Him and I returned to Him because I am God—the second Person of the Trinity.

I entered your world to provide a way for you to have a living, eternal relationship with your Father-God. People who do not know Me have often stated that there are many ways to God. But this claim is absolutely untrue: *I am the Way, the Truth, and the Life. No one comes to the Father except through Me.*

I come to *you*, beloved, *full of grace*. Because you have trusted Me to save you from your sins through My sacrificial death on the cross, you have nothing to fear. You don't need to dread failure or performing below expectations. Since I am your Savior—and you cannot save yourself—your security rests in My grace. Rejoice that I am both faithful and sufficient. In spite of all the trouble in this world, *in Me you may have Peace. I have overcome the world*!

The Word became flesh and made his
dwelling among us. We have seen his glory,
the glory of the One and Only, who came
from the Father, full of grace and truth.

JOHN 1:14

Jesus said to him, "I am the way, the truth, and the
life. No one comes to the Father except through Me."

JOHN 14:6 NKJV

"I have told you these things, so that in me you may
have peace. In this world you will have trouble.
But take heart! I have overcome the world."

JOHN 16:33

I am the Lord of Peace. I give you Peace at all times and in every way. There is a deep, gaping hole within you that can be filled only by My peaceful Presence. People who don't know Me try to fill that emptiness in many different ways, or they simply pretend it isn't there. Even My children often fail to recognize the full extent of their need: *at all times* and in every situation. But recognizing your neediness is only half the battle. The other half is to believe I can—and will—supply all you need.

Shortly before My death, I promised Peace to My disciples—and to all who would become My followers. I made it clear that this is a gift: something I provide freely and lovingly. So your responsibility is to *receive* this glorious gift, acknowledging to Me not only your need but also your desire. Then wait expectantly in My Presence, ready to receive My Peace in full measure. If you like, you can express your openness by saying, "Jesus, I receive Your Peace."

Now may the Lord of peace himself give you peace at all times and in every way. The Lord be with all of you.

2 THESSALONIANS 3:16

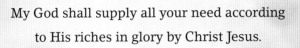

My God shall supply all your need according to His riches in glory by Christ Jesus.

PHILIPPIANS 4:19 NKJV

Let the peace of Christ rule in your hearts, since as members of one body you were called to peace. And be thankful.

COLOSSIANS 3:15

"Peace I leave with you; my *peace* I give you. I do not give to you as the world gives. Do not let your *hearts* be troubled and do not be afraid."

JOHN 14:27

I WANT YOU TO KNOW the depth and breadth of *My Love that surpasses knowledge*. There is an enormous difference between knowing Me and knowing *about* Me. Similarly, experiencing My loving Presence is vastly different from knowing facts about My character. To experience My Presence, you need the empowering work of My Spirit. Ask Him to *strengthen you with Power in your inner being* so that you can *know My Love* in full measure.

Since the moment of your salvation, I have been alive in your heart. The more room you make for Me there, the more I can fill you with My Love. There are several ways to expand this space in your heart. It's crucial to take time with Me—enjoying My Presence and studying My Word. It is also vital to stay in communication with Me. As the apostle Paul wrote, *pray continually*. This joyful practice will keep you close to Me. Finally, let My Love flow through you to others—in both your words and your actions. This *makes My Love in you complete*.

I pray that out of his glorious riches he may strengthen
you with power through his Spirit in your inner being, so
that Christ may dwell in your hearts through faith. And I
pray that you, being rooted and established in love, may
have power, together with all the saints, to grasp how wide
and long and high and deep is the love of Christ, and to
know this love that surpasses knowledge—that you may
be filled to the measure of all the fullness of God.

EPHESIANS 3:16–19

And there is salvation in no one else; for there is
no other name under heaven that has been given
among men by which we must be saved.

ACTS 4:12 NASB

Dear friends, since God so loved us, we also ought to love
one another. No one has ever seen God; but if we love one
another, God lives in us and his love is made complete in us.

1 JOHN 4:11–12

Pray

continually.

1 THESSALONIANS 5:17

I AM WORTHY of all your confidence, all your trust. So refuse to let world events spook you. Instead, pour your energy into trusting Me and looking for evidence of My Presence in the world. Whisper My Name to reconnect your heart and mind to Me quickly. *I am near to all who call upon Me.* Let Me wrap you up in My abiding Presence and comfort you with My Peace.

Remember that I am both loving and faithful. *My Love reaches to the heavens, My faithfulness to the skies*! This means you can never come to the end of My Love. It is limitless and everlasting. Moreover, you can stand on the Rock of My faithfulness, no matter what circumstances you may be facing.

People routinely put their confidence in their abilities, education, wealth, or appearance. But I urge you to place your confidence fully in Me—the Savior whose sacrificial death and miraculous resurrection opened the way for you into *eternal Glory*!

The LORD is near to all who call upon Him,
to all who call upon Him in truth.

PSALM 145:18 NKJV

Your love, O LORD, reaches to the heavens,
your faithfulness to the skies.

PSALM 36:5

For our light and momentary troubles are achieving
for us an eternal glory that far outweighs them all.

2 CORINTHIANS 4:17

I have called you by name; you are Mine. No matter how isolated you may sometimes feel, you belong to Me! I have redeemed you by paying the full penalty for your sins. *Nothing can separate you from My loving Presence.* I called you to Myself in the most personal way: reaching down into the circumstances of your life, speaking into the intricacies of your heart and mind. Although I have vast numbers of followers, you are not a number to Me. I always speak to you *by name*. In fact, you are so precious to Me that *I have inscribed you on the palms of My hands.*

When world events are swirling around you and your personal world feels unsteady, don't let your mind linger on those stressors. Tell yourself the truth: "Yes, this world is full of trouble, but Jesus is with me and He is in control." It is this *but Jesus* factor that makes all the difference in your life. Change the subject from problems to My Presence many times daily by whispering, "But Jesus . . ." and looking to Me.

The Lord who created you, O Israel, says: Don't be afraid, for I have ransomed you; I have called you by name; you are mine.

ISAIAH 43:1 TLB

I am convinced that neither death nor life, neither angels nor demons, neither the present nor the future, nor any powers, neither height nor depth, nor anything else in all creation, will be able to separate us from the love of God that is in Christ Jesus our Lord.

ROMANS 8:38–39

"See, I have inscribed you on the palms of My hands; your walls are continually before Me."

ISAIAH 49:16 NKJV

*T*RUST ME IN THE DEPTHS of your being. It is there that I live in constant communion with you. When you feel flustered and frazzled on the outside, do not get upset with yourself. You are only human, and the swirl of events going on all around you will sometimes feel overwhelming. Rather than scolding yourself for your humanness, remind yourself that I am both with you and within you.

I am with you at all times, encouraging and supportive rather than condemning. I know that deep within you, where I live, My Peace is your continual experience. Slow down your pace of living for a time. Quiet your mind in My Presence. Then you will be able to hear Me bestowing the resurrection blessing: *Peace be with you.*

To them God has chosen to make known among the Gentiles the glorious riches of this mystery, which is Christ in you, the hope of glory.

COLOSSIANS 1:27

"And teaching them to obey everything I have commanded you. And surely I am with you always, to the very end of the age."

MATTHEW 28:20

On the evening of that first day of the week, when the disciples were together, with the doors locked for fear of the Jews, Jesus came and stood among them and said, "Peace be with you!"

JOHN 20:19

ASTE AND SEE THAT I AM GOOD. The more intimately you experience Me, the more convinced you become of My goodness. I am *the Living One who sees you* and longs to participate in your life. I am training you to find Me in each moment—to be increasingly aware of My loving Presence. Sometimes My blessings come to you in mysterious ways: through pain and trouble. At such times you can know My goodness only through your trust in Me. Understanding will fail you, but trust will keep you close to Me.

Thank Me for the gift of My Peace, a gift of such immense proportions that you cannot fathom its depth or breadth. When I appeared to My disciples after the resurrection, it was Peace that I communicated first of all. I knew this was their deepest need: to calm their fears and clear their minds. I also speak Peace to you, for I know your anxious thoughts. Listen to Me! Tune out other voices so that you can hear Me more clearly. I designed you to dwell in Peace all day, every day. Draw near to Me; receive My Peace.

Taste and see that the LORD is good; blessed
is the man who takes refuge in him.

PSALM 34:8

So she called the name of the Lord Who spoke
to her . . . [the Living One Who sees me].

GENESIS 16:13−14 AMP

On the evening of that first day of the week, when the disciples
were together, with the doors locked for fear of the Jews, Jesus
came and stood among them and said, "Peace be with you!"

JOHN 20:19

*P*UT YOUR HOPE IN ME, and My *unfailing Love will rest upon you*. Some of My children have forgotten how to hope. They have been disappointed so many times that they don't want to risk being let down again. So they forge ahead stoically—living mechanically. Other people put their hope in problem solving, the stock market, the lottery, and so on. But I challenge you to place your hope fully in *Me*.

No matter what is happening in your life now, your story has an amazingly happy ending. Though the way ahead may look dark to you, there is brilliant, everlasting Light at the end of your earth-journey. My finished work on the cross secured this heavenly hope for you, and it is absolutely assured. Moreover, knowing that your story finishes well can fill your present journey with Joy. The more you put your hope in Me, the more My Love-Light shines upon you—brightening your day. Remember that I am with you continually, and I Myself *am* your Hope!

We wait in hope for the Lord; he is our help and our shield. In him our hearts rejoice, for we trust in his holy name. May your unfailing love rest upon us, O Lord, even as we put our hope in you.

PSALM 33:20–22

A faith and knowledge resting on the hope of eternal life, which God, who does not lie, promised before the beginning of time.

TITUS 1:2

Paul, an apostle of Jesus Christ, by the commandment of God our Savior and the Lord Jesus Christ, our hope.

1 TIMOTHY 1:1 NKJV

Your longing for heaven is good because it is an extension of your yearning for Me. The hope of heaven is meant to strengthen and encourage you, filling you with wondrous Joy. Many Christians have misunderstood this word *hope*, believing that it denotes wishful thinking. Nothing could be further from the truth! As soon as I became your Savior, heaven became your ultimate destination. The phrase *hope of heaven* highlights the benefits you can enjoy even while remaining on earth. This hope keeps you spiritually alive during dark times of adversity; it brightens your path and heightens your awareness of My Presence. My desire is *that you may overflow with hope by the power of the Holy Spirit.*

Not only so, but we ourselves, who have the firstfruits of the Spirit, groan inwardly as we wait eagerly for our adoption as sons, the redemption of our bodies. For in this hope we were saved. But hope that is seen is no hope at all. Who hopes for what he already has? But if we hope for what we do not yet have, we wait for it patiently.

ROMANS 8:23–25

God did this so that, by two unchangeable things in which it is impossible for God to lie, we who have fled to take hold of the hope offered to us may be greatly encouraged. We have this hope as an anchor for the soul, firm and secure. It enters the inner sanctuary behind the curtain.

HEBREWS 6:18–19

May the God of hope fill you with all joy and peace as you trust in him, so that you may overflow with hope by the power of the Holy Spirit.

ROMANS 15:13

*Y*OU ARE NO STRANGER TO ME, dear one. *Before I formed you in the womb I knew you.* My knowledge of you has continued without interruption: through your entrance into this world and onward throughout your life. I delight in transforming you more and more into the one I created you to be, much as a skilled potter delights in the work he is creating.

One implication of My uninterrupted Presence with you is that you are never alone. I am training you to be increasingly aware of Me, but I understand that you are human and your attention span is limited. Sometimes when you are suffering, you may feel as if you're alone or abandoned. However, I suffered alone on the cross so that you would *never* have to be alone in your struggles. *You are always with Me; I hold you by your right hand.*

The last enemy you will face is death, but My crucifixion and resurrection have decimated that foe! So trust Me to guide you through your life, and *afterward take you into Glory.*

"Before I formed you in the womb I knew you, before you were born I set you apart; I appointed you as a prophet to the nations."

JEREMIAH 1:5

Your eyes saw my unformed body. All the days ordained for me were written in your book before one of them came to be.

PSALM 139:16

Yet I am always with you; you hold me by my right hand. You guide me with your counsel, and afterward you will take me into glory.

PSALM 73:23—24

Rejoice and exult in hope; be steadfast and *patient* in suffering and tribulation; be *constant* in prayer.

ROMANS 12:12 AMP

*R*EJOICE AND EXULT IN HOPE. Raise a shout of Joy! You have good reason to be joyful, because you're on your way to heaven. I have paid the penalty for your sins and clothed you in My own righteousness. *This* is the basis of hope—for you, for all who truly know Me as Savior. No matter what is going on in your life at this time, your hope in Me is secure. No one will be able to *snatch you out of My hand*. In Me you have absolute, eternal security!

Be constant in prayer—at all times, but especially when you are struggling. During trials, you need close communication with Me more than ever. However, your ability to concentrate may be hampered by stress and fatigue. So make full use of the amazing source of strength within you—My Spirit. Ask the Holy Spirit to *control your mind*: to think through you and pray through you. Your prayers need not be pretty or proper. Just let them flow out of your current situation. As you stay in communication with Me, I help you to be *steadfast and patient in suffering*.

For the grace of God that brings salvation has
appeared to all men. . . . while we wait for
the blessed hope—the glorious appearing of
our great God and Savior, Jesus Christ.

TITUS 2:11, 13

"I give [My followers] eternal life, and
they shall never perish; neither shall
anyone snatch them out of My hand."

JOHN 10:28 NKJV

The mind of sinful man is death, but the mind
controlled by the Spirit is life and peace.

ROMANS 8:6

*I*F I AM FOR YOU, *who can be against you?* Beloved, I most assuredly *am* for you since you are My follower. Of course, this doesn't mean that no one will ever oppose you. It means that having Me on your side is the most important fact of your existence. Regardless of what happens in your life, you are on the winning side! I already won the victory through My death and resurrection. I am the eternal Victor, and you share in My triumph—no matter how much adversity you encounter on your journey to heaven. Ultimately, nothing and no one can prevail against you because you belong to Me forever.

Knowing that your future is utterly secure can change your perspective dramatically. Instead of living in defensive mode—trying desperately to protect yourself from suffering—you learn to follow Me boldly, wherever I lead. I am training you not only to *seek My Face* and follow My lead but to enjoy this adventure of abandoning yourself to Me. Remember: I am your *ever-present Help in trouble*.

What, then, shall we say in response to this?
If God is for us, who can be against us?

ROMANS 8:31

When You said, "Seek My face," my heart
said to You, "Your face, LORD, I will seek."

PSALM 27:8 NKJV

God is our refuge and strength,
an ever-present help in trouble.

PSALM 46:1

*A*s you sit quietly in My Presence, let Me fill your heart and mind with thankfulness. This is the most direct way to achieve a thankful stance. If your mind needs a focal point, gaze at My Love poured out for you on the cross. Remember that *nothing in heaven or on earth can separate you from that Love*. This remembrance builds a foundation of gratitude in you, a foundation that circumstances cannot shake.

As you go through this day, look for tiny treasures strategically placed along the way. I lovingly go before you and plant little pleasures to brighten your day. Look carefully for them, and pluck them one by one. When you reach the end of the day, you will have gathered a lovely bouquet. Offer it up to Me with a grateful heart. Receive My Peace as you lie down to sleep, with thankful thoughts playing a lullaby in your mind.

For I am convinced that neither death nor life, neither
angels nor demons, neither the present nor the future,
nor any powers, neither height nor depth, nor anything
else in all creation, will be able to separate us from
the love of God that is in Christ Jesus our Lord.

ROMANS 8:38–39

For no one can lay any foundation other than
the one already laid, which is Jesus Christ.

1 CORINTHIANS 3:11

You have filled my heart with greater joy than when their
grain and new wine abound. I will lie down and sleep in
peace, for you alone, O LORD, make me dwell in safety.

PSALM 4:7–8

I HAVE GOOD PLANS FOR YOU: I offer you *hope and a future*. Many people fear the future, but ultimately yours is glorious—beyond anything you can imagine! Knowing that you are on your way to heaven is immensely important for your well-being. This knowledge can help you every day, every moment of your life. Though your residence in paradise is in the future, heavenly Light transcends time and shines upon you even in the present.

Because I paid the penalty for your sins, I am your Hope— and I will never let you down. No matter what is happening in your life, it is still realistic to *hope in Me*. If you persist in trusting Me no matter what, *you will again praise Me for the help of My Presence*. Moreover, you can anticipate, via faith, the blessing that is ahead of you and start praising Me even in the dark. As you keep looking to Me in hope, My heavenly Light shines more brightly in your heart. This is *the Light of the knowledge of My Glory*!

"For I know the plans I have for you," declares the LORD, "plans to prosper you and not to harm you, plans to give you hope and a future."

JEREMIAH 29:11

Why are you in despair, O my soul? And why have you become disturbed within me? Hope in God, for I shall again praise Him for the help of His presence.

PSALM 42:5 NASB

It is the God who commanded light to shine out of darkness, who has shone in our hearts to give the light of the knowledge of the glory of God in the face of Jesus Christ.

2 CORINTHIANS 4:6 NKJV

*T*HANK ME THROUGHOUT THIS DAY for My Presence and My Peace. These are gifts of supernatural proportions. Ever since the resurrection, I have comforted My followers with these messages: *Peace be with you*, and *I am with you always*. Listen as I offer you My Peace and Presence in full measure. The best way to receive these glorious gifts is to thank Me for them.

It is impossible to spend too much time thanking and praising Me. I created you first and foremost to glorify Me. Thanksgiving and praise put you in proper relationship with Me, opening the way for My riches to flow into you. As you thank Me for My Presence and Peace, you appropriate My richest gifts.

While they were still talking about this, Jesus himself stood among them and said to them, "Peace be with you."

LUKE 24:36

"And teaching them to obey everything I have commanded you. And surely I am with you always, to the very end of the age."

MATTHEW 28:20

Through Jesus, therefore, let us continually offer to God a sacrifice of praise—the fruit of lips that confess his name.

HEBREWS 13:15

*Y*OU ARE A DELIGHT TO ME! I know you find it difficult to receive this blessing. It is based on the unconditional Love I have for all of My followers. I love you more than you can begin to imagine, so just relax in the Light of My Presence—and take time to soak in this luminous Love. Relax with Me and listen while I *rejoice over you with singing.*

Living in a fallen world is a constant challenge. There is brokenness all around you, as well as within you. Each moment, you can choose to focus on what is wrong or to *seek My Face* and enjoy My approval. Even in the midst of important activities, you can breathe this short prayer: "I seek *You,* Jesus."

Remember that My delight in you is based on My finished work on the cross. So don't fall into the trap of trying to earn My Love. Instead, live as the one you truly are—My beloved—and let your gratitude keep you close to Me, eager to follow wherever I lead. I delight in you!

The LORD your God is with you, he is mighty to save.
He will take great delight in you, he will quiet you
with his love, he will rejoice over you with singing.

ZEPHANIAH 3:17

The Lord make His face to shine upon and enlighten you
and be gracious (kind, merciful, and giving favor) to you;
the Lord lift up His [approving] countenance upon you and
give you peace (tranquility of heart and life continually).

NUMBERS 6:25–26 AMP

When You said, "Seek My face," my heart
said to You, "Your face, LORD, I will seek."

PSALM 27:8 NKJV

But I trust in
your *unfailing* love;
my heart rejoices
in your *salvation*.
I will sing to the LORD,
for he has been *good* to me.

PSALM 13:5–6

THANK ME FOR THE GLORIOUS GIFT of forgiveness. I am your Savior-God, and I alone can give you this blessing. I went to exorbitant expense to procure this gift for you. You receive forgiveness and become My child by *receiving Me* and *believing in My Name*. This Name, Jesus, means *the Lord saves*. To receive this gift of salvation, you need to trust Me as your only Hope—the One who delivers you from all your sins.

There is no condemnation for those who are in Me. I want you to enjoy the wonder of walking through your life as My follower—totally forgiven! The best response to this wondrous gift is to live in gratitude, seeking to please Me above all else. You don't need to do good things to secure My Love, because it's already yours. Just let your desire to please Me flow readily out of your grateful heart. Thanking Me frequently will help you stay close to Me, ready to follow wherever I lead. Rejoice, beloved, for *through Me the law of the Spirit of Life has set you free*!

Yet to all who received him, to those who believed in his name, he gave the right to become children of God.

JOHN 1:12

And there is salvation in no one else; for there is no other name under heaven that has been given among men by which we must be saved.

ACTS 4:12 NASB

Therefore, there is now no condemnation for those who are in Christ Jesus, because through Christ Jesus the law of the Spirit of life set me free from the law of sin and death.

ROMANS 8:1–2

Let the *peace* of Christ
rule in your hearts,
to which indeed
you were *called* in one
body; and be thankful.

COLOSSIANS 3:15 NASB

*F*ROM THE FULLNESS OF M*Y* GRACE, *you have received one blessing after another.* Stop for a moment, beloved, and ponder the astonishing gift of salvation—*by grace through faith in Me.* Because it's entirely a gift—*not as a result of works*—this salvation is secure. Your part is just to receive what I accomplished for you on the cross, believing with the faith that was given you. This undeserved Love and favor is yours forever. My grace has infinite value!

Multiple blessings flow out of grace because of its extraordinary fullness. Guilt feelings melt away in the warm Light of My forgiveness. Your identity as a *child of God* gives your life meaning and purpose. Relationships with other people improve as you relate to them with love and forgiveness.

The best response to My bountiful grace is a heart overflowing with gratitude. Take time each day to think about and thank Me for blessings in your life. This protects your heart from weeds of ingratitude that spring up so easily. *Be thankful!*

From the fullness of his grace we have
all received one blessing after another.

JOHN 1:16

For by grace you have been saved
through faith. And this is not your own
doing; it is the gift of God, not a result
of works, so that no one may boast.

EPHESIANS 2:8–9 ESV

Yet to all who received him, to those
who believed in his name, he gave the
right to become children of God.

JOHN 1:12

*W*HEN I JOINED THE RANKS of humanity, born into the humblest conditions, My Glory was hidden from all but a few people. Occasionally, streaks of Glory shone out of Me, especially when I began to do miracles. Toward the end of My life, I was taunted and tempted to display more of My awesome Power than My Father's plan permitted. I could have called down legions of angels to rescue Me at any point. Imagine the self-control required of a martyr who could free Himself at will! All of this was necessary to provide the relationship with Me that you now enjoy. Let your life become a praise song to Me by proclaiming My glorious Presence in the world.

This, the first of his miraculous signs, Jesus performed at Cana in Galilee. He thus revealed his glory, and his disciples put their faith in him.

JOHN 2:11

The people stood watching, and the rulers even sneered at him. They said, "He saved others; let him save himself if he is the Christ of God, the Chosen One." The soldiers also came up and mocked him. They offered him wine vinegar.

LUKE 23:35–36

It is good to praise the LORD and make music to your name, O Most High, to proclaim your love in the morning and your faithfulness at night, to the music of the ten-stringed lyre and the melody of the harp. For you make me glad by your deeds, O LORD; I sing for joy at the works of your hands. How great are your works, O LORD, how profound your thoughts!

PSALM 92:1–5

I BROADEN THE PATH BENEATH YOU *so that your ankles do not turn*. This shows how intricately I am involved in your life-journey. I know exactly what is before you, and I can alter the path ahead of you to make your way easier. Sometimes I enable you to see what I have done on your behalf. At other times you are blissfully unaware of the hardship I have spared you. Either way, My work to widen the way before you demonstrates how lovingly I am involved in your life.

From your perspective, My workings are often mysterious. I do not protect you—or anyone—from *all* adversity. Neither was *I* shielded from hardship during my thirty-three years of living in your world. On the contrary, I willingly suffered unimaginable pain, humiliation, and agony on the cross—for your sake! When My Father turned away from Me, I experienced unspeakable suffering. But because I was willing to endure that excruciating isolation from Him, you will *never* have to suffer alone. I have promised: *I am with you always!*

And about the ninth hour Jesus cried out with a loud
voice, saying, "Eli, Eli, lama sabachthani?" that is,
"My God, My God, why have You forsaken Me?"

MATTHEW 27:46 NKJV

". . . And teaching them to obey everything I
have commanded you. And surely I am with
you always, to the very end of the age."

MATTHEW 28:20

You broaden the path beneath me,
so that my ankles do not turn.

PSALM 18:36

I AM THE RESURRECTION AND THE LIFE; all lasting Life emanates from Me. People search for life in many wrong ways: chasing after fleeting pleasures, accumulating possessions and wealth, trying to deny the inevitable effects of aging. Meanwhile, I freely offer abundant Life to everyone who turns toward Me. As you *come to Me and take My yoke upon you*, I fill you with My very Life. This is how I choose to live in the world and accomplish My purposes. This is also how I bless you with *Joy unspeakable and full of Glory.* The Joy is Mine, and the Glory is Mine; but I bestow them on you as you live in My Presence—inviting Me to live fully in you.

"Come to me, all you who are weary and burdened, and I will give you rest. Take my yoke upon you and learn from me, for I am gentle and humble in heart, and you will find rest for your souls."

MATTHEW 11:28–29

Whom having not seen, ye love; in whom, though now ye see him not, yet believing, ye rejoice with joy unspeakable and full of glory: Receiving the end of your faith, even the salvation of your souls.

1 PETER 1:8–9 KJV

Jesus said to her, "I am the resurrection and the life. He who believes in me will live, even though he dies."

JOHN 11:25

*A*S YOU COME TO KNOW ME more intimately, you grow increasingly aware of your sins. This presents you with a choice: to focus on your flaws and failures or to rejoice in My glorious gift of salvation. When you keep your focus on my sacrifice for your sins, you live in the joyful awareness that you are wonderfully loved. There is *no greater Love than Mine*, and it is yours forever! The best response to such a fathomless gift is to *love Me with all your heart*.

Tragically, many people think they have little—or even nothing—for Me to forgive. They've been deceived by the prevailing lie that there is no absolute truth. They believe good and evil are relative terms, so they see no need for a Savior. These deluded ones do not seek My forgiveness, and their sins remain unpardoned. The evil one's deceptions have darkened their minds. But *I am the Light of the world*, and My Light can shine through you into their lives. Because you are My follower, *you never walk in darkness—you have the Light of Life!*

But I trust in your unfailing love; my heart rejoices in your salvation. I will sing to the Lord, for he has been good to me.

PSALM 13:5–6

"Greater love has no one than this, than to lay down one's life for his friends."

JOHN 15:13 NKJV

Jesus replied, "'Love the Lord your God with all your heart and with all your soul and with all your mind.' This is the first and greatest commandment. And the second is like it: 'Love your neighbor as yourself.'"

MATTHEW 22:37–39

When Jesus spoke again to the people, he said, "I am the *light* of the world. Whoever *follows* me will never walk in darkness, but will have the light of *life*."

JOHN 8:12

*Y*OU CAN TRUST THE ONE who died for you. In this world of spin and scams, people often find it hard to believe anyone. They talk about requiring others to "earn" their trust by proving themselves. *I* am the quintessential Person who has earned the right to be trusted. For your sake, I left the glorious perfection of heaven and began life in your world as a helpless, stable-born infant. I resisted all temptations for thirty-three years so that My sacrifice for sinners would be sufficient. I lived a perfect life and freely gave My body to be tortured and executed—to pay the full penalty for sin. As a result of My death and resurrection, *whoever believes in Me has eternal Life!*

I want you to rely confidently on Me—not only as your Savior but also as the God-Friend who is taking care of you. I have already proved how trustworthy I am. Now I invite you to relax in My loving Presence and confide in Me. Tell Me your hopes and fears. *Cast all your anxiety on Me because I care for you.*

For you know the grace of our Lord Jesus Christ, that though He was rich, yet for your sakes He became poor, that you through His poverty might become rich.

2 CORINTHIANS 8:9 NKJV

Whoever believes in the Son has eternal life, but whoever rejects the Son will not see life, for God's wrath remains on him.

JOHN 3:36

Cast all your anxiety on him because he cares for you.

1 PETER 5:7

"Come to me, all you
who are *weary* and burdened,
and I will give you *rest*."

MATTHEW 11:28

TAKE HOLD OF THE HOPE THAT I OFFER TO YOU—and *be greatly encouraged.* The hope of heaven is your birthright as a Christian. Many, many blessings flow out of that glorious promise into your present life in this world. Notice, however, that *take hold* is an active verb—requiring effort on your part. As the apostle Paul taught, you need to *press on toward the goal and live up to what you have already attained.* This requires you to exert yourself—grasping onto the heavenly hope from which so many blessings flow.

One of those blessings is encouragement. *Be encouraged* is a passive form of the verb. You receive encouragement as a free gift from Me when you make the effort to hold on to your hope—focusing on what I've *already* done (died for your sins), what I *am* doing (living in you), and what I *will* do (take you home to heaven). I love to give good gifts in generous proportions. So cling to hope, beloved, and you will be *greatly* encouraged.

God [confirmed his promise to Abraham] so that, by
two unchangeable things in which it is impossible
for God to lie, we who have fled to take hold of the
hope offered to us may be greatly encouraged.

HEBREWS 6:18

I press on toward the goal to win the prize for which God
has called me heavenward in Christ Jesus. All of us who are
mature should take such a view of things. And if on some
point you think differently, that too God will make clear to
you. Only let us live up to what we have already attained.

PHILIPPIANS 3:14—16

I have been crucified with Christ; it is no longer I
who live, but Christ lives in me; and the life which
I now live in the flesh I live by faith in the Son of
God, who loved me and gave Himself for me.

GALATIANS 2:20 NKJV

He saved us, not because of *righteous* things we had done, but because of his *mercy*. He saved us through the washing of rebirth and *renewal* by the Holy Spirit.

TITUS 3:5

I AM A GOD WHO GIVES and gives and gives. When I died for you on the cross, I held back nothing; I poured out My Life *like a drink offering*. Because giving is inherent in My nature, I search for people who are able to receive in full measure. To increase your intimacy with Me, the two traits you need the most are receptivity and attentiveness. Receptivity is opening up your innermost being to be filled with My abundant riches. Attentiveness is directing your gaze to Me, searching for Me in all your moments. It is possible to *stay your mind on Me*, as the prophet Isaiah wrote. Through such attentiveness you receive a glorious gift: My perfect Peace.

But even if I am being poured out like a drink offering on the sacrifice and service coming from your faith, I am glad and rejoice with all of you.

PHILIPPIANS 2:17

"I tell you the truth, anyone who will not receive the kingdom of God like a little child will never enter it."

MARK 10:15

You will keep him in perfect peace, whose mind is stayed on You, because he trusts in You.

ISAIAH 26:3 NKJV

OU ARE NOT YOUR OWN, for you were bought with a price. And that price was exorbitant—My very Life! I went through excruciating pain and humiliation as I sacrificed Myself for your sins. This was a gift of infinite value—an act of indescribable Love. However, only those who recognize their sinfulness, their need for a Savior, can receive this astonishing gift of Love. Hear My invitation calling out: *"Come to Me, all you who are weary and burdened, and I will give you rest."* Sin is a terrible, crushing burden, but I have paid the price *in full* to remove it from you forever.

When you awaken each morning, say to yourself: "I am not my own. I belong to Jesus." Then keep in mind Whose you are as you make your way through the day, especially as you make plans and decisions. Knowing that you belong to Me helps you keep your feet on *the path of Peace.* This knowledge meets deep-seated needs. You can find spiritual and emotional security by remembering that you are *Mine*—My beloved.

Or do you not know that your body is a temple of the Holy Spirit within you, whom you have from God? You are not your own, for you were bought with a price. So glorify God in your body.

1 Corinthians 6:19–20 ESV

And you, my child, will be called a prophet of the Most High; for you will go on before the Lord to prepare the way for him, to give his people the knowledge of salvation through the forgiveness of their sins, because of the tender mercy of our God, by which the rising sun will come to us from heaven to shine on those living in darkness and in the shadow of death, to guide our feet into the path of peace.

Luke 1:76–79

"Come to me, all you who are weary and burdened, and I will give you rest."

Matthew 11:28

*S*OMETIMES YOUR JOURNEY through this world is wearisome. You feel as if you've been plodding uphill wearing leaden clothing, and you don't want to take another step. At such times you need to stop and re-center your thoughts on Me. Remember that I am your constant Companion, eager to help you take the next step—and then the next. You have to take only one at a time! Instead of staring grimly into the future, dreading the journey ahead of you, direct your focus to the present and to My Presence with you.

As you walk with Me along your life-path, let the hope of heaven shine brightly on you, lighting up your perspective dramatically. Though the way ahead may be steep and difficult, the end of your journey is stunningly glorious—beyond description! And every moment you are getting closer to your heavenly home. As you look to Me in faith—trusting in My finished work on the cross—the Light of heaven's hope shines upon you and brightens the path just before you.

For we were saved in this hope, but hope that is seen is not hope; for why does one still hope for what he sees? But if we hope for what we do not see, we eagerly wait for it with perseverance.

ROMANS 8:24–25 NKJV

The Lord will rescue me from every evil deed and bring me safely into his heavenly kingdom. To him be the glory forever and ever.

2 TIMOTHY 4:18 ESV

Blessed are those who have learned to acclaim you, who walk in the light of your presence, O LORD.

PSALM 89:15

Y CHILDREN make a pastime of judging one another—and themselves. But I am the only capable Judge, and I have acquitted you through My own blood. Your acquittal came at the price of My unparalleled sacrifice. That is why I am highly offended when I hear My children judge one another or indulge in self-hatred.

If you live close to Me and absorb My Word, the Holy Spirit will guide and correct you as needed. There is *no condemnation* for those who belong to Me.

He saved us, not because of righteous things we had done, but because of his mercy. He saved us through the washing of rebirth and renewal by the Holy Spirit.

TITUS 3:5

Now there is in store for me the crown of righteousness, which the Lord, the righteous Judge, will award to me on that day—and not only to me, but also to all who have longed for his appearing.

2 TIMOTHY 4:8

Therefore, there is now no condemnation for those who are in Christ Jesus.

ROMANS 8:1

"Do not *judge*, and you will not be judged. Do not *condemn*, and you will not be condemned. *Forgive*, and you will be forgiven."

LUKE 6:37

*Y*OU OVERWHELMINGLY CONQUER *through Me*, the King of Glory who loves you. No matter what is happening in this fractured, fallen world or in your own life, you are victorious. I won the Victory once for all time through My sacrificial death and miraculous resurrection. *My unfailing Love* has accomplished this wondrous conquest and made you much, much more than a conqueror. You're an heir of the kingdom of eternal Life and Light!

Nothing will be able to separate you from My Love! Ponder what it means to have *Me* as the Lover of your soul every moment, forever and ever. Your soul is the eternal part of you, the part that can never be separated from Me. It is not what you see in the mirror or what other people reflect back to you. It is the essence of who you are—the "real you" that is *being transformed from Glory to Glory.* Therefore, do not be discouraged by the defects you see in yourself. Instead, remember that you are continually being *transformed into My image*—and rejoice!

But in all these things we overwhelmingly conquer through Him who loved us. For I am convinced that neither death, nor life, nor angels, nor principalities, nor things present, nor things to come, nor powers, nor height, nor depth, nor any other created thing, will be able to separate us from the love of God, which is in Christ Jesus our Lord.

ROMANS 8:37–39 NASB

But I trust in your unfailing love; my heart rejoices in your salvation. I will sing to the Lord; for he has been good to me.

PSALM 13:5–6

But we all, with unveiled face, beholding as in a mirror the glory of the Lord, are being transformed into the same image from glory to glory, just as by the Spirit of the Lord.

2 CORINTHIANS 3:18 NKJV

*L*ET ME FILL YOU WITH MY JOY AND PEACE. They flow into you as you sit quietly in My Presence, trusting Me in the depths of your being. These blessings are essential for nourishing your soul. *The Joy of the Lord is your strength*, so don't neglect this delightful gift. It is for all times and all circumstances, though sometimes you have to search for it. You also need My Peace at all times, and I bestow it on you freely as you trust in Me.

Remember that I am *the God of hope*. The hope I offer is not wishful thinking. It is absolutely certain, even though it refers to things not yet fully realized. It is utterly secure because I Myself obtained it through My finished work on the cross. This hope is the foundation of the Joy and Peace you find in Me. No matter how hard your life may be at this time, you have full assurance that endless delight awaits you in heaven, where I have *prepared a place for you*. As you ponder this glorious truth, you can enjoy hope that *overflows by the Power of the Holy Spirit*.

May the God of hope fill you with all joy and peace
as you trust in him, so that you may overflow
with hope by the power of the Holy Spirit.

ROMANS 15:13

Then [Nehemiah] said to [all the people of Israel], "Go your
way, eat the fat, drink the sweet, and send portions to those
for whom nothing is prepared; for this day is holy to our Lord.
Do not sorrow, for the joy of the LORD is your strength."

NEHEMIAH 8:10 NKJV

"In My Father's house are many mansions; if it were not so, I
would have told you. I go to prepare a place for you. And if I
go and prepare a place for you, I will come again and receive
you to Myself; that where I am, there you may be also."

JOHN 14:2–3 NKJV

I AM THE RISEN ONE who shines upon you always. You worship a living Deity, not some idolatrous, man-made image. Your relationship with Me is meant to be vibrant and challenging as I invade more and more areas of your life. Do not fear change, for I am making you a *new creation, with old things passing away and new things continually on the horizon.* When you cling to old ways and sameness, you resist My work within you. I want you to embrace all that I am doing in your life, finding your security in Me alone.

It is easy to make an idol of routine, finding security within the boundaries you build around your life. Although each day contains twenty-four hours, every single one presents a unique set of circumstances. Don't try to force-fit today into yesterday's mold. Instead, ask Me to open your eyes so you can find all I have prepared for you in this precious day of Life.

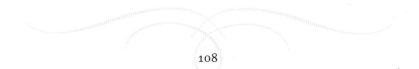

The angel said to the women, "Do not be afraid, for I know that you are looking for Jesus, who was crucified. He is not here; he has risen, just as he said. Come and see the place where he lay. Then go quickly and tell his disciples: 'He has risen from the dead and is going ahead of you into Galilee. There you will see him.' Now I have told you."

MATTHEW 28:5–7

He tends his flock like a shepherd: He gathers the lambs in his arms and carries them close to his heart; he gently leads those that have young.

ISAIAH 40:11

Therefore, if anyone is in *Christ*,
he is a new *creation*; the old
has gone, the *new* has come!

2 CORINTHIANS 5:17

*H*EAVEN IS both present and future. As you walk along your life-path holding My hand, you are already in touch with the essence of heaven: nearness to Me. You can also find many hints of heaven along your pathway because the earth is radiantly alive with My Presence. Shimmering sunshine awakens your heart, gently reminding you of My brilliant Light. Birds and flowers, trees and skies evoke praises to My holy Name. Keep your eyes and ears fully open as you journey with Me.

At the end of your life-path is an entrance to heaven. Only I know when you will reach that destination, but I am preparing you for it each step of the way. The absolute certainty of your heavenly home gives you Peace and Joy to help you along your journey. You know that you will reach your home in My perfect timing: not one moment too soon or too late. Let the hope of heaven encourage you as you walk along the path of Life with Me.

But Christ has indeed been raised from the dead, the firstfruits of those who have fallen asleep. For since death came through a man, the resurrection of the dead comes also through a man. For as in Adam all die, so in Christ all will be made alive. But each in his own turn: Christ, the firstfruits; then, when he comes, those who belong to him.

1 CORINTHIANS 15:20–23

We have this hope as an anchor for the soul, firm and secure. It enters the inner sanctuary behind the curtain.

HEBREWS 6:19

*F*IND YOUR SECURITY IN ME. As the world you inhabit seems increasingly unsafe, turn your attention to Me more and more often. Remember that I am with you at *all* times, and I have already won the ultimate victory. Because *I am in you and you are in Me*, you have an eternity of perfect, stress-free life awaiting you. There will be no trace of fear or worry in heaven. Reverential worship of *the King of Glory* will flood you with unimaginable Joy!

Let this *future hope* strengthen and encourage you while you're living in this deeply fallen world. When you start to feel anxious about something you have seen, heard, or thought, bring that concern to Me. Remind yourself that *I* am the One who makes you secure—in all circumstances! If you find your mind gravitating toward an idolatrous way of feeling safe, tell yourself: *"That's* not what makes me safe." Then look trustingly to Me, and think about who I am: the victorious Savior-God who is your Friend forever. In Me you are absolutely secure!

"On that day you will realize that I am in my Father, and you are in me, and I am in you."

JOHN 14:20

Lift up your heads, O you gates! And be lifted up, you everlasting doors! And the King of glory shall come in.

PSALM 24:7 NKJV

There is surely a future hope for you, and your hope will not be cut off.

PROVERBS 23:18

*C*OME TO ME AND LISTEN! Attune yourself to My voice, and receive My richest blessings. Marvel at the wonder of communing with the Creator of the universe while sitting in the comfort of your home. Kings who reign on earth tend to make themselves inaccessible; ordinary people almost never gain an audience with them. Even dignitaries must plow through red tape and protocol in order to speak with royalty.

Though I am King of the universe, I am totally accessible to you. I am with you wherever you are. Nothing can separate you from My Presence! When I cried out from the cross, *"It is finished!" the curtain of the temple was torn in two from top to bottom.* This opened the way for you to meet Me face to Face, with no need of protocol or priests. I, the King of kings, am your constant Companion.

"Why spend money on what is not bread, and your labor on what does not satisfy? Listen, listen to me, and eat what is good, and your soul will delight in the richest of fare. Give ear and come to me; hear me, that your soul may live. I will make an everlasting covenant with you, my faithful love promised to David."

ISAIAH 55:2–3

When he had received the drink, Jesus said, "It is finished." With that, he bowed his head and gave up his spirit.

JOHN 19:30

And when Jesus had cried out again in a loud voice, he gave up his spirit. At that moment the curtain of the temple was torn in two from top to bottom. The earth shook and the rocks split.

MATTHEW 27:50–51

The Sovereign Lord has given me an instructed tongue, to know the word that *sustains* the weary. He wakens me morning by morning, wakens my ear to *listen* like one being taught.

ISAIAH 50:4

*R*EJOICE THAT YOUR NAME IS WRITTEN *in heaven*—in the book of Life. Because you are Mine, you have Joy that is independent of circumstances. You have received eternal Life that will *never* be taken away from you. *Those who are justified* (through faith in Me as their risen Savior) *are also glorified.* There is a very real sense in which you are already *seated with Me in the heavenly realms.*

Joy is the birthright of all who belong to Me. It can coexist with the most difficult, heartrending circumstances. So come to Me each morning with open hands and an open heart, saying, "Jesus, I receive your Joy." Then wait with Me while the Light of My Presence shines upon you—soaking into the depths of your inner being. Thus I strengthen you, preparing you for the day that stretches out before you.

As you journey through this day, return to Me for fresh Joy as often as you need. I am a God of unlimited abundance, so I always have more than enough for you.

"However, do not rejoice that the spirits submit to you, but rejoice that you names are written in heaven."

LUKE 10:20

❧

And those he predestined, he also called; those he called, he also justified; those he justified, he also glorified.

ROMANS 8:30

❧

And God raised us up with Christ and seated us with him in the heavenly realms in Christ Jesus.

EPHESIANS 2:6

*H*OPE FOR WHAT YOU DO NOT SEE; *eagerly wait for it with perseverance*. Among the five senses, sight is often the one that people value the most. I created the world gloriously beautiful, and I want you to appreciate beauty when you see it. However, even more beneficial than sight is hope, which is itself a kind of vision. It enables you to see—through the eyes of your heart—things that are *not yet*. The most stunning example of this is the hope of heaven. Your ultimate destiny is to share in My Glory! This is My promise to you, secured through My finished work on the cross and My resurrection.

Practice hoping for things you do not see—both for this life and the next. Ask Me to guide you into hopes and dreams that are in line with My will. Train the eyes of your heart to "see" these blessings, while praying for My will to be done fully and only. Discipline yourself to *wait eagerly*—with your focus on Me and the longed-for outcome. Remain hopeful and expectant as you *wait with perseverance*.

If we hope for what we do not see, we
eagerly wait for it with perseverance.

ROMANS 8:25 NKJV

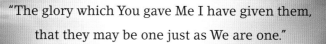

"The glory which You gave Me I have given them,
that they may be one just as We are one."

JOHN 17:22 NKJV

Now faith is the assurance (the confirmation, the title
deed) of the things [we] hope for, being the proof of things
[we] do not see and the conviction of their reality [faith
perceiving as real fact what is not revealed to the senses].

HEBREWS 11:1 AMP

Those who look
to him are *radiant*;
their faces are never
covered with shame.

*B*ASK IN THE LUXURY of being fully understood and unconditionally loved. Dare to see yourself as I see you: radiant in My righteousness, cleansed by My blood. I view you as the one I created you to be, the one you will be in actuality when heaven becomes your home. It is My Life within you that is changing you *from glory to glory*. Rejoice in this mysterious miracle! Thank Me continually for the amazing gift of My Spirit within you.

Try to depend on the help of the Spirit as you go through this day of life. Pause briefly from time to time so you can consult with this Holy One inside you. He will not force you to do His bidding, but He will guide you as you give Him space in your life. Walk along this wondrous way of collaboration with My Spirit.

God made him who had no sin to be sin for us, so that in him we might become the righteousness of God.

2 CORINTHIANS 5:21

But we all, with unveiled face, beholding as in a mirror the glory of the Lord, are being transformed into the same image from glory to glory, just as by the Spirit of the Lord.

2 CORINTHIANS 3:18 NKJV

Since we live by the Spirit, let us keep in step with the Spirit.

GALATIANS 5:25

EVEN THOUGH YOU DO NOT SEE ME, you believe in Me. I am far more real—complete, unchanging, unlimited—than the things you can see. When you believe in Me, you are trusting in rock-solid Reality. I am the indestructible *Rock* on which you can keep standing, no matter what your circumstances may be. And because you belong to Me, I am devoted to you. Beloved, I encourage you to *take refuge in Me.*

Believing in Me has innumerable benefits. The most precious one is *the salvation of your soul*—forever and ever. Your belief in Me also enhances your present life immensely, making it possible for you to know who you are and Whose you are. As you stay in communication with Me, I help you find your way through this fallen world with hope in your heart. All of this enlarges your capacity for Joy. The more you seek Me and the more fully you know Me, the more I can fill you with *inexpressible and glorious Joy!*

Though you have not seen him, you love him;
and even though you do not see him now, you
believe in him and are filled with an inexpressible
and glorious joy, for you are receiving the goal
of your faith, the salvation of your souls.

1 PETER 1:8–9

The LORD is my rock, my fortress and my deliverer;
my God is my rock, in whom I take refuge. He is my
shield and the horn of my salvation, my stronghold.

PSALM 18:2

But if we hope for what we do not see, we
eagerly wait for it with perseverance.

ROMANS 8:25 NKJV

A CHEERFUL HEART IS GOOD MEDICINE. You have every reason to be cheerful because *I have overcome the world. I have conquered it and deprived it of power to harm you* through My victory on the cross. Moreover, nothing you will ever encounter along your life-path *will be able to separate you from My Love.* As you ponder these glorious truths about all I have done for you, let *good cheer* fill your heart and radiate from your face.

A joyful heart will improve your health—spiritually, emotionally, and physically. So fill your mind with thankful thoughts till your heart overflows with Joy. Take time to praise Me for all that I am—the One from whom all blessings flow. Let Me fill you with My Light and Life, for I designed you to be full of heavenly contents. As these divine nutrients soak into the depths of your being, they strengthen you and enhance your health. *Be of good cheer!*

A cheerful heart is good medicine, but
a crushed spirit dries up the bones.

PROVERBS 17:22

"I have told you these things, so that in Me you
may have [perfect] peace and confidence. In the
world you have tribulation and trials and distress
and frustration; but be of good cheer [take courage;
be confident, certain, undaunted]! For I have
overcome the world. [I have deprived it of power
to harm you and have conquered it for you.]"

JOHN 16:33 AMP

Neither height nor depth, nor anything else in
all creation, will be able to separate us from the
love of God that is in Christ Jesus our Lord.

ROMANS 8:39

I *delight* greatly in the LORD; my soul rejoices in my God. For he has *clothed* me with garments of salvation and arrayed me in a robe of *righteousness*, as a bridegroom adorns his head like a priest, and as a bride adorns herself with her *jewels*.

ISAIAH 61:10

WHEN YOUR SINS WEIGH HEAVILY upon you, come to Me. Confess your wrongdoing, which I know all about before you say a word. Stay in the Light of My Presence, receiving forgiveness, cleansing, and healing. Remember that *I have clothed you in My righteousness*, so nothing can separate you from Me. Whenever you stumble or fall, I am there to help you up.

Man's tendency is to hide from his sin, seeking refuge in the darkness. There he indulges in self-pity, denial, self-righteousness, blaming, and hatred. But *I am the Light of the world*, and My illumination decimates the darkness. Come close to Me and let My Light envelop you, driving out darkness and permeating you with Peace.

But if we walk in the light, as he is in the light, we have fellowship with one another, and the blood of Jesus, his Son, purifies us from all sin.

1 JOHN 1:7

I delight greatly in the LORD; my soul rejoices in my God. For he has clothed me with garments of salvation and arrayed me in a robe of righteousness, as a bridegroom adorns his head like a priest, and as a bride adorns herself with her jewels.

ISAIAH 61:10

When Jesus spoke again to the people, he said, "I am the light of the world. Whoever follows me will never walk in darkness, but will have the light of life."

JOHN 8:12

I AM ABLE to *keep you from stumbling.* I know how weak you are, how easily you would lose your footing if I were not holding onto you. You are *growing in grace,* but complete freedom from sin will not be possible as long as you live in this fallen world. So you need My help continually.

I am able to *present you faultless*—blameless, perfect, unblemished—*before the Presence of My Glory* because *I have clothed you with garments of salvation and arrayed you in a robe of righteousness.* I want you to wear these royal raiments with confidence. You are absolutely secure because it is *My* righteousness that saves you, not yours.

Exceeding Joy is for you and for Me. I delight in you now, but this Joy will be immeasurably magnified when you join Me in Glory. The jubilation you will experience in heaven is indescribable—far beyond any pleasure you could know in this world. Nothing can rob you of this glorious *inheritance that can never perish, spoil, or fade!*

Now to Him who is able to keep you from stumbling, and to present you faultless before the presence of His glory with exceeding joy, to God our Savior, who alone is wise, be glory and majesty, dominion and power, both now and forever. Amen.

JUDE VV. 24–25 NKJV

⟨⟨◯⟩

But grow in the grace and knowledge of our Lord and Savior Jesus Christ. To him be glory both now and forever! Amen.

2 PETER 3:18

⟨⟨◯⟩

Praise be to the God and Father of our Lord Jesus Christ! In his great mercy he has given us new birth into a living hope through the resurrection of Jesus Christ from the dead, and into an inheritance that can never perish, spoil or fade—kept in heaven for you.

1 PETER 1:3–4

I BROUGHT YOU OUT INTO A SPACIOUS PLACE; *I rescued you because I delighted in you.* No matter what your circumstances, if you belong to Me, you are in *a spacious place* of salvation. You may be feeling cramped in your current situation, but your salvation is an ever-expanding gift. My Spirit lives inside you, and He is always working to sanctify you—making you more like Me. This is an inner expansion, and it will continue till I call you home *to Glory.*

Heaven is a wondrously spacious place; you will never feel cramped or frustrated there. *I will wipe away every tear* from the eyes of My people. There will be *no more death, nor sorrow, nor crying*, and *no more pain.* Everything and everyone in heaven will be perfect. My limitless ocean of Love will wash over you and fill you to overflowing. You will finally be able to love Me—and other people—with perfect Love untainted by sin. This heavenly experience will continue to expand in ever-increasing gladness throughout eternity!

He brought me out into a spacious place; he
rescued me because he delighted in me.

2 SAMUEL 22:20

You guide me with your counsel, and
afterward you will receive me to glory.

PSALM 73:24 ESV

And I heard a loud voice from heaven saying, "Behold,
the tabernacle of God is with men, and He will dwell
with them, and they shall be His people. God Himself
will be with them and be their God. And God will wipe
away every tear from their eyes; there shall be no
more death, nor sorrow, nor crying. There shall be no
more pain, for the former things have passed away."

REVELATION 21:3—4 NKJV

I GIVE YOU MY SHIELD OF VICTORY, *and My right hand sustains you.* I won the ultimate victory through My sacrificial crucifixion and My miraculous resurrection! I did this for *you,* for all who trust Me as Savior-God. I accomplished everything! Your part is just to *believe:* that you need a Savior to pay the penalty for your sins and that *I* am the only Way of salvation.

Your saving faith sets you on a path to heaven. Meanwhile, My victorious shield protects you as you journey through this world. Use *the shield of faith to stop the fiery arrows of the devil.* When you're in the thick of battle, call out to Me: "Help me, Lord! I trust in *You.*"

As you live in close dependence on Me, My right hand does indeed sustain you, holding you up. I have indescribably great Power! Yet I use My mighty right hand not only to protect you but to tenderly lead you and help you keep going. Sometimes I even *gather you in My arms and carry you close to My heart.*

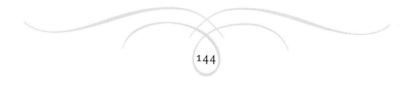

You give me your shield of victory, and your right hand sustains me; you stoop down to make me great.

PSALM 18:35

Jesus said to him, "I am the way, the truth, and the life. No one comes to the Father except through Me."

JOHN 14:6 NKJV

In addition to all of these, hold up the shield of faith to stop the fiery arrows of the devil.

EPHESIANS 6:16 NLT

He tends his flock like a shepherd: He *gathers* the lambs in his arms and carries them close to his heart; he *gently* leads those that have young.

ISAIAH 40:11

I AM ALWAYS AVAILABLE TO YOU. Once you have trusted Me as your Savior, I never distance Myself from you. Sometimes you may *feel* distant from Me. Recognize that as feeling; do not confuse it with reality. The Bible is full of My promises to be with you always. As I assured Jacob, when he was journeying away from home into unknown places, *I am with you and will watch over you wherever you go.* After My resurrection, I made this promise to My followers: *Surely I am with you always, to the very end of the age.* Let these assurances of My continual Presence fill you with Joy and Peace. No matter what you may lose in this life, you can never lose your relationship with Me.

"Though the mountains be shaken and the hills be removed, yet my unfailing love for you will not be shaken nor my covenant of peace be removed," says the LORD, who has compassion on you.

ISAIAH 54:10

"I am with you and will watch over you wherever you go, and I will bring you back to this land. I will not leave you until I have done what I have promised you."

GENESIS 28:15

"Therefore go and make disciples of all nations, baptizing them in the name of the Father and of the Son and of the Holy Spirit, and teaching them to obey everything I have commanded you. And surely I am with you always, to the very end of the age."

MATTHEW 28:19–20

I WANT YOU TO DRAW WATER *from the wells of salvation with Joy.* These wells are unfathomably deep, and they are filled to the brim with My blessings. The worth of your salvation is inestimable, far greater than all of earth's fortunes—past, present, and future. When your life in this world ends, you will live with Me *forever* in a perfect environment filled with dazzling Glory. You will worship Me with untold numbers of My followers, all of whom will relate to one another with wondrous Love—and respond to Me with even *greater* Love. Moreover, you will be able to receive Love from Me in unimaginably great measure!

The assurance of forevermore-pleasures awaiting you in heaven can help you endure your struggles in this world. I understand the difficulties you're facing, but remember: I am *your Strength and Song.* I am strong enough to carry you when you feel as if you can go no further. I even enable you to sing with Me—on good days *and* hard days. I, *your Song,* can fill you with Joy!

Surely God is my salvation; I will trust and not
be afraid. The LORD, the LORD, is my strength
and my song; he has become my salvation.

ISAIAH 12:2–3

For you know the grace of our Lord Jesus Christ, that
though he was rich, yet for your sakes he became poor,
so that you through his poverty might become rich.

2 CORINTHIANS 8:9

You will show me the path of life; in Your
presence is fullness of joy; at Your right
hand are pleasures forevermore.

PSALM 16:11 NKJV

I AM CHRIST IN YOU, THE HOPE OF GLORY. The Messiah—the Savior of the world—lives in you! This promise is for all who have faith in Me: I *dwell in your hearts through faith.* This amazing blessing is a work of My Spirit in your inner being. The more you trust Me, the more you can enjoy My indwelling Presence—and the more effectively I can live through you.

In a world that may seem increasingly hopeless, remember that I am *the hope of Glory.* This hope is ultimately about heaven, where you will live with Me forever. But the Light of heaven's Glory is so brilliant that some of its rays can reach you even in the present—no matter how dark your circumstances may appear. I am *the Light that shines on in the darkness, for the darkness has never overpowered it.* As you follow Me along your life-path, clothed in My righteousness, this Light *shines brighter and brighter until full day.*

God has chosen to make known among the
Gentiles the glorious riches of this mystery,
which is Christ in you, the hope of glory.

COLOSSIANS 1:27

I pray that out of his glorious riches he may strengthen
you with power through his Spirit in your inner being,
so that Christ may dwell in your hearts through faith.

EPHESIANS 3:16—17

The path of the righteous is like the light of dawn,
which shines brighter and brighter until full day.

PROVERBS 4:18 ESV

The Light shines on in the darkness, for the darkness has never overpowered it [put it out or absorbed it or appropriated it].

JOHN 1:5 AMP

I AM ALL AROUND YOU, hovering over you even as you seek My Face. I am nearer than you dare believe, closer than the air you breathe. If My children could only recognize My Presence, they would never feel lonely again. *I know every thought before you think it, every word before you speak it.* My Presence impinges on your innermost being. Can you see the absurdity of trying to hide anything from Me? You can easily deceive other people, and even yourself, but I read you like an open, large-print book.

Deep within themselves, most people have some awareness of My imminent Presence. Many people run from Me and vehemently deny My existence because My closeness terrifies them. But My own children have nothing to fear, for I have cleansed them by My blood and clothed them in My righteousness. Be blessed by My intimate nearness. Since I live in you, let Me also live through you, shining My Light into the darkness.

O Lord, you have searched me and you know me. You know when I sit and when I rise; you perceive my thoughts from afar. You discern my going out and my lying down; you are familiar with all my ways. Before a word is on my tongue you know it completely, O Lord.

PSALM 139:1–4

But now in Christ Jesus you who once were far away have been brought near through the blood of Christ.

EPHESIANS 2:13

God made him who had no sin to be sin for us, so that in him we might become the righteousness of God.

2 CORINTHIANS 5:21